Of Me and You

Poems and illustrations by Eva Halus

Of Me and You
Poems 2010-2013

Author: Eva Halus
Illustrations: Eva Halus
Photo on front cover: "Magical Attraction", acrylics on cardboard by Eva Halus
(2005)

Editors: Ruxandra Vidu and Ioana Ene

COPYRIGHT 2014 © REFLECTION PUBLISHING

Reflection Publishing
P.O. Box 2182
Citrus Heights, California 95611-2182
E-mail: info@reflectionbooks.com

www.reflectionbooks.com

ISBN: 978-1-936629-32-9

First Edition

Printed in the United States of America

Preface

Motto: "Ut pictura poesis", Horace (65 - 8 B.C.)

I don't shrink away from confessing that I like Eva's poetry as well as her paintings, so, it's a pleasure to sit down at my writing table and to pen a few thoughts about this last book of hers. As this moment is a sort of festivity for me I have to put on my silk and satins-silken slippers, too and start (not to forget my cup of coffee, exquisite).

Miss Eva Halus is an industrious young woman who works a lot both as a teacher of painting, a studio painter and, of course, in spare time, as a poetess, successful in both fields. I think Horace's saying «Ut pictura poesis» (a poem is like a painting) appeals very well to Eva's preoccupations.

If we add Paul Valery's remark: «de la musique avant tout» we have the two basics of a classical poem: image and sounding. Of course our poetess knows those things very well and she proves it in her works-past and present!

I have in front of me a bunch of more than sixty poems adorned by illustrations made by Eva herself, poems different as lengths, mostly love poems (it's normal thinking of the author's age-but there are many exceptions, too, Goethe, Hardy, myself) all written in a fine, clear and unique style.

The volume opens with «Introduction of the author» (to the one that prepares to read my book) - a bitter-hilarious remark, isn't it) - followed by a rather short text in which she points out some philosophical ideas with hints to two olden philosophers: Aristotle and Plato (one materialistic, the other is the father of world idealism; one praising matter, the other the idea). The volume, as it is, starts with a fresh, perfumed poem called Magical Attraction, containing wide cosmic views of the nature embedded with philosophy, too, of universal attraction.

I quote:

> *«Like the chrysanthemum*
>
> *Like the humming bird*
>
> *And earth and sun*
>
> *That attract each other*
>
> *And like a human to another*
>
> *We live the rules of complementaries.»*

The poem ends with an emblematic stanza:

> *«I›m the painter who works*
>
> *Under the blue and pale yellow*
>
> *And meets the philosophy*
>
> *Of being you, of being me.»*

Telepathy is a nice, strange poem telling a charming love story-a mixture of religious philosophy,

> *«From the myriads of stars,*
>
> *Slowly waltzing over the sea*
>
> *One detaches and from its brightness*
>
> *A young prince descends.*
>
> *Who is he?*
>
> *I'm the one from nameless places*
>
> *That no human eye did see...» etc.*

Then a dialogue follows between the young prince from above and the wise man.

The young man concludes like this:

> *«Please, don't disturb the order that*
>
> *Is given by the hands of God,*
>
> *Telepathy comes along just when*
>
> *You perceive your Lord, Amen!»*

This volume contains memorable lines, let's quote some of them, at random: «From the sweet, passion and sorrow / I make my coronet for tomorrow». These are a fine couplet of classical verses, or, on another page: «Like me or not / That's who I am». Or furthermore: «The silky blue skies / This curtain of my eyes». These two verses end the poem «Don't give up! (of love and revolution).

«A story of two worlds» is a real success, too: it opens with a nice, panoramic image, like a dreamlike painting. I quote:

> *Moon rises over the hills*
>
> *And reflexes in the wavy lake*
>
> *Mirroring the dale,*
>
> *Round and gloomy;*
>
> *Time for a tale*
>
> *The stars told me»…*

…and a fantastic story happens in the universe. The poem is rather long, ending such as follows:

> *«The morning star*
>
> *Closely twinkles*
>
> *And I say gently:*

Oh, Cavalier of the sky

Will your Universe

Glitter with laughs

Across the world

That just began?»

Another interesting fragment of a poem:

«And when the sun shines

A whole garden of the soul shines (...)

And when the lights are on

I still can see myself

As part of the game,

But now the stage is restrained

To paper and pen.»

Of course, now is the moment when the poetess plans writing her gracious poems. «The Midday Angel» is a clear love poem achieved with some subtle artistic means:

«When I sleep

He brings me all my friends

Wishing me

The Midnight Angel

To be in love.»

A very strange love poem is that entitled: «Advice» (a poem written at Christmas Time):

The night was deep, no stars,

Just the yellow stone began to shine

And my answer was:

«Unless I›m a princess of another kind

I want him, I want my own child!»

A very moving, strange poem, with a mysterious rugged visitor, on Christmas night, strange indeed.

The book is illustrated with a number (some 14-15 in all) of meaningful images made by the author's hand. The illustrations bring a variation and «respiro» to the readers. Of course, this book contains a lot of other poems, being worth mentioning, but we'll put an end, by letting the readers to discover far more pleasures in this volume. The majority of the poems in this volume are written in English, except the last nine poems of which, most of them are wonderful ones especially: Japanese Landscape and Remembering a berry tree-all these poems are translated from Romanian.

Now, to end with, here is the first stanza from the poem «If trees had memories», that, we think, speaks for itself.

«Big trees, hundreds of years

Still bearing elastic branches

Adorned with greenly-loved leaves,

Yellow buds which come with the spring

To fully grown-up leaves-dark-green

Lit up red before they disappear.

If they had memories...

They could tell

Who lived, who passed away...»

Yes, indeed, they would be some good, truthful chroniclers of past times.

That's all from my part now, I honestly invite the good reader to take a look over this fine book, hoping it won't be a waste of time...

Traian Gardus *- poet, epigrammatist and English teacher*

Introduction of the author*

I opened my heart as a book-

- It's written in riddles

With roses dew and blood-

And has thorns,

You think you can read in its pages

As the eye uncovers

It's petals one by one...

Only One knows to read it!

All others are just screeching

The surface of the glass

That guards my book open

In the open light of my thought

Making me tremble, making me kneel

To the roots of my rose,

Inside of me, free

From the screeching world at last!

I opened my heart as a book

But my silence grew faster

Surrounding me with bits of cotton -

- The willow buds -

My darling from afar...

To heal my flower from the noise outside!

I opened my heart as a book

Willing the Sun to salute

And embrace the World

As a lost, lonely friend,

Not knowing that

The World will be willing to devour it

In its madness imploring for goods.

To the One that prepares to read my book

If you and I, sorry if you or I have to ponder upon this book from a philosophical point of view, the following quote from Jostein Gaarder`s book «Sophie`s World» is totally relevant about the point of view you and I shall adopt reading these poems. If you let me do this comparison, me, the author could be Aristotle or Plato, or both in turn, or I could be one of them and you, the reader, the other one. It is not for sure which one of them had it right, but I am inclined to leave you with their arguing conversation on the subject. While reading my poems you will find yourself merged into this kind of controversy. I will leave up to the reader to make the final decision, or you may find that the truth lies in between:

«But you should not ignore the fact that this is a dramatic turn of thought. The highest degree of reality in Plato`s theory, was that in which we think with our reason. It was equally apparent to Aristotle that the highest degree of reality is that in which we perceive with our senses. Plato thought that all the things existed in the higher reality of the world of ideas and thereby in the human soul. Aristotle thought the opposite: things that are in the human soul were purely reflections of natural objects. So nature is the real world. According to Aristotle, Plato was trapped in a mythical world picture in which the human imagination was confused with the real world. So, Aristotle pointed out that nothing exists in consciousness that has not first been experienced by the senses.

Plato would have said that there is nothing in the natural world that has not first existed in the world of ideas. Aristotle held the thought that Plato was «doubling the number of things». He explained a horse by referring to the «idea» of a horse. But what kind of explanation is that, Sophie? Where does the «idea» of a horse come from, is my question. Might there not even be a third horse, which of the «idea» horse is just an imitation? Aristotle did not deny that humans have innate reason. On the contrary, it is precisely reason, according to Aristotle, that is man`s most distinguishing characteristic. But our reason is completely empty until we have sensed something. So man does not have innate ideas».

Rose, *acrylics on rice paper (2000)*

Miracle flower

«Liberty» she said,

But she was thinking just at freedom

In a state of mind

That she considered prison.

Somehow she locks herself

In prescribed patterns

Of each culture that matters

For each, but not for everybody...

In the midst of discovering

A new way of wondering,

After years of experiences

Where nothing was proved:

People just fashioning,

She takes a chance for empowering

Herself with no other than solitude

And, thus, she expects discovering

Her own ways-writing the Modern Bible

Of her own days.

Is that an Angel sitting beside her?

One by one, days with

Angels, or Demons, or Animals, or People,

Or just Nothingness: the gift of emptiness

Take their turn in guiding her

In a universe that matters.

Hangover with Civilization,

Different parts of consciousness

Cling to different acts,

With different parts of people and city,

In different pacts.

It's like running on lethal stairs

That led nowhere.

It's like we are in a very high, empty pot-

- You have to build something

To pull you over its edges:

Ah, the Miracle Flower Forever!

Its blossoms already cook in the pot

Desires, smelling of freedom.

It's veins sport over its edges

The few interested in escalating

Surroundings, taking some glimpses

To...each other!

(Nobody else addresses a look

Over their noses

Being absorbed in details

Of their own branches,

Too tingled and long

To be considered by others.)

The Miracle Flower Forever!

Ah, her blossom- the Dream that awakes

The Angels of Heaven

To walk by you

In the realm of the Real,

Proof print of the Beginning of Life

Pure, sound and joy,

Like no Other

Earth that you ever imagined!

Magical Attraction, *acrylics on cardboard (2001)*

Magical attraction

Huge chrysanthemum

Habituates her brain,

Her thoughts, her actions

Are all petals vibrating serene.

She grew up as a flower

Her intuition is the cup of Heaven

In the shadow

Her head-a chrysanthemum

Is glowing pale and yellow,

Her face and neck are blue

As the untouched yet sky.

From above

A hummingbird gently picks

From distant skies;

It is just a man in disguise

Who thought to reach the suave flower

In promise of love and power.

Magical Attraction

Of opposites

Of elements which tell

In their embodiment

A story that spurs in its refinement.

Like the chrysanthemum

Like the humming bird

And earth and sun

That attract each other

And like a human to another

We live the rule of complementaries

That complete each other

Like the common one and the other.

Pale yellow and deep blue

At the heart of my view,

I take my paints

And I enter the mystery

Of translating this image

Into a still-life coverage.

Tiger and cubs, *acrylics on wood (2005)*

Telepathy

From the myriads of stars

Slowly waltzing over the sea

One detaches and from its brightness

A young prince descends;

Who is he?

«I'm the one from nameless places

Whom no human eye did see

Thinking deep as night

Over the human history.

I see from my silent Universe

Children sometimes pointing at me

Butterflies and lions hunting

In the forest until they reach the sea.

I would like to talk your language

But it's like a bee zooming to me,

I came a long way just to tell you

The truth about the universal language

That is telepathy.

«In ancient times silently watching the skies

The wise man understood that in the dark

The light passes and encompasses

Communication rule for humans, too.»

The wise man deeply thought

And in the realm of clearer thought,

An impulse like a bit of light

Caught his inner eye.

«We can communicate like stars,

Our sensors will tell us all»,

The ancient thought.

«Telepathy» the wise man said

Should be our nature of the future», but then

The prince from high above replied:

«You better understand

That every animal and plant

Are sharing the same light from the sun

And are arranged in harmony

By their degree of sanctity.

Please, don't disturb the order that

Is given by the hands of God.

Telepathy comes along just when

You perceive your Lord. Amen!»

A story of two worlds

Moon rises over the hills

And reflexes in the wavy lake

Mirroring the dale

Round and gloomy,

Time for a tale

The stars told me:

«You will see from the right star

Descending on a ray of light

A cavalier of the skies,

Across the valley.»

The clock tiny tocks in the room,

Seconds suspended

Silence demanding.

A knock in the window:

The cavalier descending

On a ray of light

Just in my window.

He reveals his front

From a cloudy clog,

It's figure in the moonlight

Is shining with an unearthly glow:

«I live across the Universe

Where I rule over three planets.

I bathe them in valleys of light,

All three, but no creature,

No sound, no birth

Ever happen to me.»

He's pale now

In the dark of my room.

Maybe the shadow

Takes his universal power;

«For an advice you came» I say,

Changing your splendor of light

Huge, by day as by night

For some earthly love

That makes our world turn on and on

And being green:

You need a seed.»

Now and then in my bed

The sun and the moons

Cosmic chemistry

Bending the power of light

Float like the first seconds of life.

Deep in a dream I drew.

When I open my eyes

The morning star

Closely twinkles

And I say gently:

«Oh, Cavalier of the sky,

Will your Universe glitter with laughs

Across the Universe in your world that just began?»

Pioneers of time, *digital image (2012)*

About beginnings

Forgotten cavaliers

Forgotten courtesy

Forgot even the sound of love-

Your voice in me,

Forgot roses in children's berlingos

Forgot smells that bring me back to you.

Where are you now?

The time elapses in spirals

Of cosmic dust,

I left you in the inner circle

Of my Universe, to last,

But the spiral evolving

Dusts new territories

Expending fast

And I can't reach the beginning,

Just new illusions, too fast.

What other circles, with other faces

Do you trust?

Forgot the beginnings,

Trust for trust?

Forgot that our love

Was a double star

Now a shadow

In hundreds of shadows

In the cold place

Where no one is visiting at last?

...I wish that the pioneers of time

Will be together till the End of Time...

Fragment of the world

Fragment of the world

Cosmos contained in all

Rose petals as the desire of soul

As fingers and toes

Rose painted by young girls;

I see the Universe in a rose.

Underneath the ants are moving to a new home

Flying ants, empresses of the land,

Bellow, my father passes in stroll,

Two species in our World.

I see he is tall

Somehow sun blends

Making him

A man filled with light.

State of trinity

One Son of our will

Two hands: one of his faith in us

The other one, our love for him.

We clasp our hands

And make love growing

LIKE THE SUN

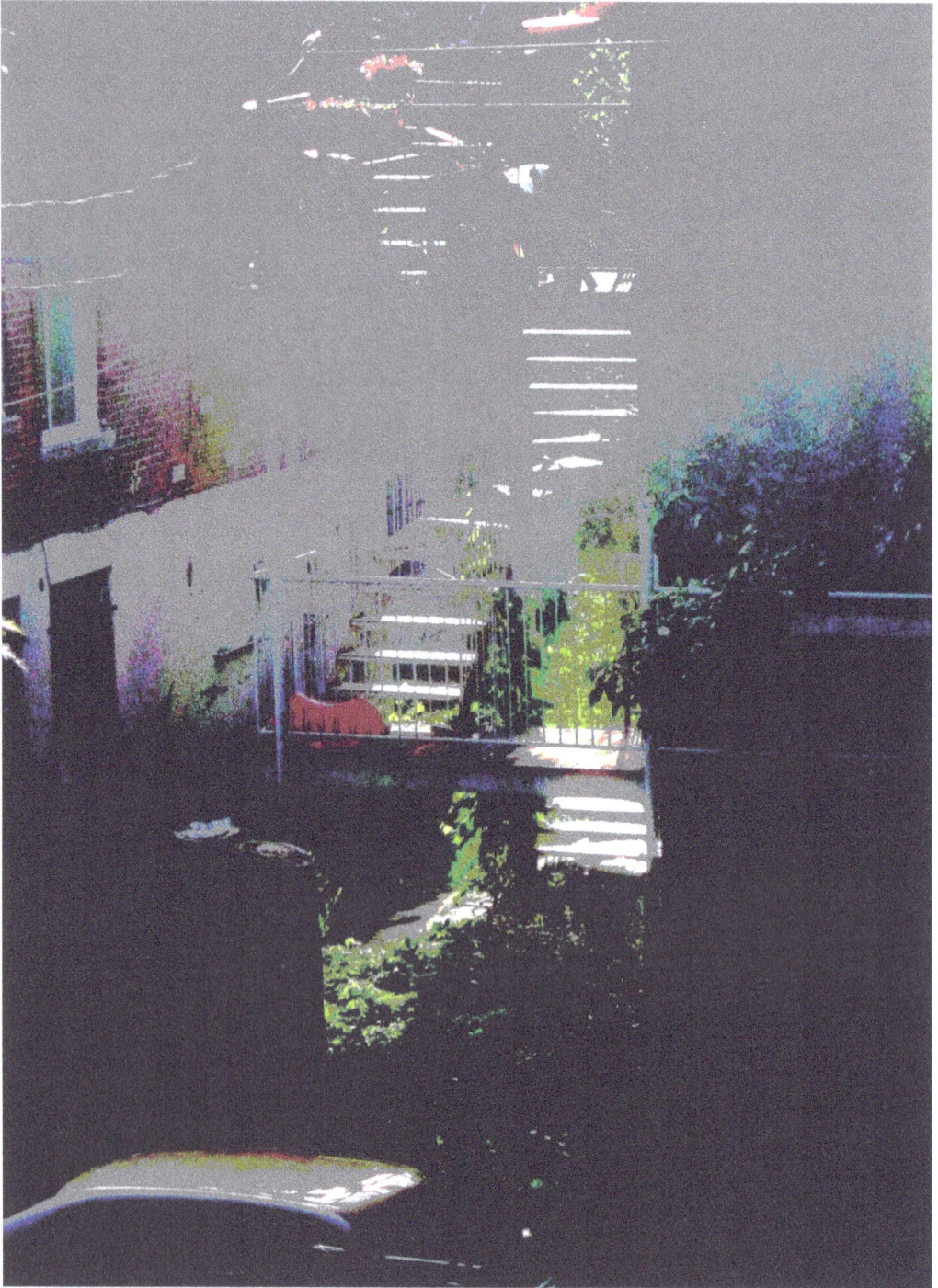

Stairway to Heaven, *photography (2012)*

Wedding in the sky

(photo: Stairway to Heaven)

Like faded stars

The sand tossed under my pace,

At the beginning of time

At the beginning of the sea

We got together-never parted.

Across the sky, another moment

Reveals the forbidden garden

Where we passed our lives,

No features, just two unknown people

That didn't kept it secret:

Loving One and love for all!

Roses will bloom

Blossoms of freedom,

Cup of Heaven will be thy Soul

Parted with the World!

Vow

Sweet arrow you launched in my dream

Awakening with it my Will.

Underneath I breathe

Not sure if I please.

Sagittarian I aim

At the world that turns like a wheel.

From the sweat, passion and sorrow

I make now my coronet for tomorrow.

Don't give up

- of love and revolution -

Reminiscence of what was stuck behind the curtain

That the Angels weaved for our love

Not to see in front what was once behind us,

Giving us the present

Always with the Flammarion of the future

In the twinkle of the eye.

A sleep of Rationality

That brought us,

The children of Normality,

And no more Monsters

Of our saddest and desperate acts

Or malformations of intentions

Never brought to happen

But desired at last.

This weight I bring with me,

This is my language,

The fireballs of my eyes,

That I bring with me

In a such a quiet, peaceful world

That we forget to breath,

Subjects of another moment

When I'm not called by my name anymore!

I don't give up

I'm just so awake

I sleep when others talk,

So «mince» when I turn to you,

So «fat» when I think out of the blue.

Like me or not

That's who I am.

The silky blue skies

This curtain of my eyes...

The Midday Angel

The Midday Angel
That I saw in the face of the Sun
Dancing in spirals of a shell,
Disappeared without a shadow
Under a curtain of rain.

He suddenly appeared
In another place
With curtains the color
Of the sea and sand,
On the 5th floor
Of a building with balconies and no door.

In my memory
Washed by the sea
When I sleep
He brings me all my friends

Wishing me
The Midnight Angel
To be in Love.

Thoughtful day

The Angel was the kindness

In a diamond wheel

Spinning joy and happiness

To whomever he pleased.

But the Amusement Park

Was closed in the rain

Carrousels stood still

The games were over

No light was shining in.

A school bus parked at the edge

Children were piercing the windows

Covered with bubbles of rain,

Nobody came out

The tickets were sold

But no one could play.

The Angel left the spinning wheel

Up on a cloud of rain

Starring with empty, glancing eyes

At the shady Park bellow.

He was whispering in the thoughts of children

A song from his youth:

«In a rainy day be merry

I will carry out the shadow

In a dark basket, making it darker

So the Sun will be free to shine

And I will turn the Diamond Wheel

Faster and faster.»

Children were a little sad

Their bus left, they-hanging

Their necks backwards-

And thinking of the Angel

That even Spirits are dark...

Who you are

Your realms of imagination

Intersected with surfaces and volumes

Of things that people had built-

-Everything before you-

Your ribs that keep your heart in a nest

Much dearer than the rest,

Your hands that touch and feel

Your reason to be here still,

Your legs that still run

For the best to be won,

Your sight cut in rare diamonds

So perfect, you don't have to blink

But you blink much, much more often

-You are to be born-

And the tears don't come:

Maybe God's eyes that don't cry.

And your realm of imagination

Intersected with will
Love and freedom,
What rare and eternal flowers
Will bring to cover
Reality in a soft grass,
Reality to be the Magic,
Where everything that man builds
Nature and you
Will move to the light pace
Of love and harmony.

Do you listen? There are just
Your ears and lips
That are fatal mischiefs
One mouth, but two ears
To listen twice as you speak.
Words don't come right,
Words bless,
Ears don't hear right
Ears hurt,
When they, instead, have to
Take the blessing of
Being the first.

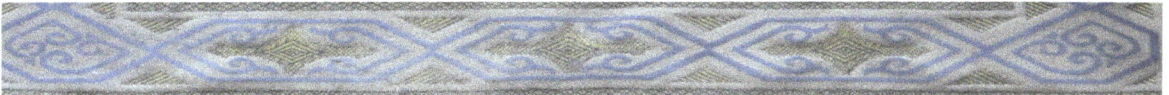

Cubist woman sawing (Tribute to Fashion Designer Oana Comsa),
acrylics on wood (2012)

Dissecting the Will

Rationality shares in equal squares

Portions of time while absorbed in details.

Solving the equations of macramé

While the beauty lies

In the inner process

Of making this tablecloth

For serving a meal,

Each plate in a square

For those who,

With the fork and knife

Will dissect the reasons

Of their own Will...

...Not knowing that the beauty stands

In the inner process

Of sharing the meal with God,

Not in the rational shares

Of portions of meat

While absorbed in the «eating»

Solving the equations

Of covering the macramé

With their plates…

…Not knowing that the beauty stands

In the inner process

Of macramé squares,

Covered with plates

From which we are eating

Sharing the meal with God!

Thoughts for sweeping the house

Tender elements of a clear day,

Some said we look forth foreseeing the rain?

Big sky, so blue-something is born here,

It's balance between good and bad.

A lot of stress contained

In unsaid parts of unwanted junk

That populates daily life

Of common sense that we became.

Old Tree on St. Michel Blvd., *photography (2012)*

If trees had memories

Big trees

Hundreds of years

Still bearing elastic branches

Adorned with greenly-loved leaves

Yellow buds that come with the spring

To fully grown-up leaves-dark-green

Lit-up red before they disappear.

If trees had memories...

They could tell

Who lived, who passed away

Or just how many times, how many years

Varvara went from home to shopping-mall

And how many children came to see her,

How many times, how long

Till she gave her last breath

In her own home

Surrounded by trees that witnessed her life all.

If trees had memories...

They could remember

The times with chariots with horses,

The first tramway

The building of Villa-Maria,

The building of democracy

And snowstorms that occurred

When foundations were not secure.

If trees could remember

I vowed love to you For Ever.

My trees from my hometown

Knew that you'll never return.

Alas, but everyday

From morning till dawn

I look around me for your signs.

The days happen one by one,

Walking, running along the clock,

Nothing stable in the process of time,

But trees will remember

Just a linear time

Photographed by them when I walk by,

That is the direction of my love to you,

To some other point in the world

Wherever you happen to be,

Whatever you do.

Seclusion to inner freedom

I secluded myself

To find out what I am

Without ribbons and fun.

I find the inner freedom

In easy steps towards my depth.

When the night is dark with no moon

I can see the strength of my will

That played to delirium the acts of life

And that I can now describe as fair.

So I secluded myself

To weight the world

In balance on my shoulders

To see again the reason to be me

With me as the soldier and lover

With me as mother and daughter

And just the Holly Father can tell

Who is what and who is when.

And when the sun shines

A whole garden of the soul shines.

And when the lights are on

I still can see myself

As a part of the Game,

But now the stage is restrained

To paper and pen.

Sunflowers

From a bee-scale-

Faces filled with seeds

Facing the sun,

The planet where I come to pray

In my garment with wings,

Me, a drone.

Golden fields

Where the world isn't born yet,

Following the sun

Every day.

From a human scale-

-Sunflowers with ten dollars,

In an entrance

And they will stay there

Till they will grow old and fanned

- Just in few days.

And the owner will

Discard them in a barrel

Labeled «Recycling», or even

In the garbage

With no mention, however,

That they were the hearts of the sun,

True pieces of life

Visiting from a far land.

With ten dollars a bouquet

I can't forget!

Bubble-bubble

Surrounded by pink

A trace of blue-

From another gum

Piercing the bubble

And a freezing green-yellow

Of my goggles emerging

From the bubble of the man

That chews pink bubble-gum

Covering the entire

Surface of the room

With illusions.

I see inside mountains and lakes

Pink craters of who was the best

Inside the game that rolled

From south to the north

Of my body in love.

A small explosion proceeds,

I am left in the room

With bits of curling pink

That eat the walls

And no one is near.

It had to happen because

He was ballooning for too long

Illusions that he was displaying

And I was just inhaling.

Bubbles-bubbles

When I will get out there

You can remember me

As a surfer of bubbles

That led just to troubles.

Advice

(poem written at Christmas Time)

The tall pilgrim bowed,

He picked a yellow pebble from the ground

And then, addressing with a smile

He said: «Don't wait for him, the Earth is round.

How many stones you saw like this?

Everything on Earth is unique.

Come, woman, with me on a Holly Trip

We'll make it holly by the people we meet

And things like these that we pick.

When we'll be achieving our trip

In the same place we will come

And you'll see these pebbles

Will be smaller and round,

Nothing on Earth stays the same over the years,

Not even your face will be in ten years so clear,

Don't worry, you'll have a child to care about

Even if it will be in the form

Of an old rugged beggar like me

Because this is the true love of Jesus Christ,

Choosing to love the Cup of Life,

Not choosing the golden recipient on a shelf

Grace for a selfish eye and mind.

The night was deep, no stars,

Just the yellow stone began to shine

And my answer was:

«Unless I'm a princess of another kind

I want him, I want my own child!»

Echo

The road is long,

So lonely and cold,

We laughed, we joked,

We spoke good words,

Just to forget it all

At the crossroad

Where we took each one

Another line

Following from there

One way direction on a split.

I never thought you are so physical,

Following your life and mine

Like geography that spreads on a map:

A mountain there, a river of tears here...

...So nobody will ever know that once

My river was the mountain's ice-cap

And since you've lost your cool with me

I cry a river of tears,

Flowing far- you melt my heart,

You disappeared from my sight,

I see just wrinkles in the Earth's crust,

In plains of grass and dust,

When once I was just home

To beautiful rocks

Pierced by holly rhododendrons

And cock-crest, weaving never good-bye,

Just singing along with the whistle of winds

Long prayers and mantras above.

Or maybe it was then your breath,

The breathing mountain of mine

That I remember now when tearing down

My way through the plains

That whistles still, in an echo, your name:

The water's memory carried away...

The coming of the age

I was the artist

Adorning your ego

With tremendous grace

With pictures sliding one to another

In fairy tales,

At your day to day pace,

Paving your way with surprises

In the form of flowers, birds and trees

And sometimes snowfalls

For you to really be.

And the people you met?

So pleasing, so truly pleased

To be with you

When you were shinning in my grace.

But you surrendered

To these times of falling grace

Lost too soon

And for too long

In a reverie that ends

In gray landscapes,

Grey eyes that watch them grey,

Grey trends,

Grey hands and hair,

Grey planes.

Is it the coming of the age

When lips don't kiss

But also hands and soul don't pray?

Abandoned empty on a lonely road,

Being so fanciful as a turkey on a silver tray

With its fried golden wings

That strangers crunch bored and boring.

Old? As far as you and me should know

I'm coming back just when...I'll take your soul!

Enjoy life

To Kiril, over the Internet

A sparrow twirls

It is your eyebrow,

I know…

That lifts to ask me

Why?

No question, dear

It's said, but mimed

Because the reason why…

The sunshine rolls,

It is your smile,

I know…

That lifts to tell me

«I'm fine».

No question, dear

Is asked, but mimed

Because this is the reason why…

…I smile.

The years go by,

This moment stays,

I know...

We are in time...

This moment lifts us

Towards the future times,

No question, dear,

Is asked, but mimed

Because this is the reason why...

...We are children in time.

"Renaissance" with cross of light in the sky,
photography reworked in Photoshop (2009)

Mona Lisa

You hide your treasures

In a smile,

The colors that painted you

Are not arbitrary,

They are the lights of Leonardo

Waiting for the spring

That he saw hidden in your smile.

Blue, brown-it is exactly

What the painter found

And once, strolling in Montreal,

I saw the city on a cloud,

Where everything was blue and brown.

The spring was coming

And in my mind

I cheered the Renaissance

On the same ground.

Enigmatic smiles of women on the street,

The merchants on St. Dennis

Praising the clients as in older times,

Coffee shops-all blue and brown

And a beret inclining and saluting me...

...When I decided to see who was its Master,

Leonardo, with a smile, was sitting there

Watching me upon a cloud

And he-all beret and smile

Was painting heavenly from Heaven

A cross of light...

Remember

Sudden steps break the silence
In the attic someone walks
In the story, suddenly people
Break through lines
And take the pose.

What is last, at least inside me
From the glowing tale I told
Frenetically loosing its edges
When intruders roll over and all
Just ignore my references?

Who remembers my compassion
That I put at work for them?
I reached love in fantastic heights
Now my tall tower has to fall
Engluted by the grey walls
Of the city within the city
Within the city, within the city...

Remember me, so I don't have to fall!

To be or not to be... a poet, *photography (2012)*

To be or not to be... a poet

I gave a part of me

In a book. I can't find you anywhere,

I've lost you in the World,

In my poems to you,

So naïve that

I was reading them loud

For ears that never heard

Your commanding voice

Interrupting me

To stop me from doing

What was close to a blasphemy,

A dissertation

Of the silent breath

Which was arousing our bodies

To the fresh air

Of real poetry

Of Nirvana.

Shakespeare, too,

Must he suffered a lot

To reveal his sonnets

To the World.

Is like as nobody knew that

Writing poems

Is to be ready to die

And be reborn

Like a Phoenix

From the ashes of your love

In the black charcoal of the words.

Shakespeare, too,

Must he suffered a lot

To reveal his poems

To the World.

But, at least, he was Shakespeare

While us, we had a meaning,

Just for me and you.

Face to face

Hello, my life,

I am alone,

How many times

Did you adorn my soul

With love, love, love?

Today we stay both again

Face to face

Contemplating a sum

Of whom I was

Of whom I am.

You don't tell me a thing,

I have to discover all alone

What hides in the wrinkles

Of a mother so old,

But in your eternal smile

I see the promise

And I feel my courage

To smile for you

Whatever mirages you plan.

The truth

I see it now:

Just what I imagine about your way

You mirror back to me

In a reminiscence of Angels

And Saints and slaves to you,

But, also, other warriors

And other people

That cheered you, too.

You show me now

Plainly, your face

In a big light

Where Heaven and Grace

Melt with the Earth

In a total embrace.

Don't scorn me mother life

I love you!

Unspoken prayer

We gathered,

It was worm.

We spoke,

Compassion was born.

We stood there together,

We ate in peace

Speaking about matters

That matter.

At the window

Pigeons gathered,

It was cold,

Winter storm,

They were maybe listening,

The spirit was listening with them

Upon us and them to be born.

It was a prayer in time,

We had it on our lips

Even if nobody spoke it,

The room with us and

Pigeons around

Was an Oasis in the winter's eye

And maybe the bigger soul of an Entity

Formed ad-hoc by a prayer of the Deity...

Pigeons on the window panel in a snowstorm, *photography (2012)*

Prayer

Many stars the sky bears

Of this cold winter in a prayer

In clear water before the dark

A girl mirrors in her palms

Many trembling stars holding with her eyes

In her palms, in water, as many stars

As a child can count.

She drinks, she says a prayer

Clear water, clear sky

The stars above touched my heart

I pray, Immaculate Mother

To be your good child.

The countless stars

Be my devotion

As far as my soul reaches

Up to the open skies.

Give me the strength to grow

To stand always for your pure soul

That is with me, and I wish one day

When I'll be grown up and strong

I can walk the path to you

With my hand in the hand of the man I'll love,

For good and for all.

St. Joseph Oratory, *oil on canvas (2011)*

Dinner at «Blanche Neige»

If you want to make me sad,

Take me to «Blanche Neige»

Give me a portion of chicken leg

Tasting very bad

Like a spell from the witch.

At home waits for me an apple -

- Red delicious…

The witch had stolen me an earring, too,

Snow White, she wasn't there, it seems

(Or she was me?)

Nor were the little dwarfs, just the cold wind

Whispering: the witch is near!

And in return, I hope another time

I'll find in my plate the ring

Of the long living prince!

Tigri

- to one of my acquaintances from ancient times -

From Pharaohs times

- And even more ancient -

She descended All Fur

To keep silence

With me, upon the secrets

Of the Sun, the Night and Heart,

Without asking a penny,

Just food and water, so far.

She is the descendent of Tigris

Her brother must have been Euphrates

Her silhouette appears in the shadow

As a thunder of my subconscious.

Silently, on her paws she enters

Through the open door

In the poetry's Spiritual World.

She, who never talks,

Who knows to be

In style and «stills»

As a real princess

Of the divine Nile.

Sleeping at my feet

She runs in dreams

That I would like to know one day,

Maybe she's dreaming of wild creatures,

About Tigris' jungle and rain,

Or maybe it is just her heart

Biting as a Tiger's

While catching the tail of a comet

Which is falling in my bed

Night after night.

My acquaintance from ancient times!

We are sometimes

At the beginning of time

Where we stitch and purr

And other times far in space

When people can't find us anywhere,

Just the moon could find us

Lost on its «other side»

In the dark, far from the sun,

Merged in real poetry...

...This is me and Tigri!

Tigri, *photography (2007)*

Flying elephant, *cartoon (2013)*

The flying elephant

(for awkward moments)

When will you stop worrying

About living, your existence?

A flying elephant

Was laughing and asked me so.

He was my dream

Moving above slow

I was following him

Just when I was hiding from you all.

Now I reveal it,

In pink and baby-blue

To laugh together

Three feet above the ground

And pat each other

For our point of view.

But sudden awkward moments come

When I touch again the ground;

It is a must for me

And I walk slowly,

Not used no more to gravity.

Scheherazade

Striving for love

The oyster shell opened bellow,

How gracefully will she punch it with the fork

Longing for the plate, from above?

Her profile, blended by the sun,

...Dolcé, shifts against blue drapes in the window,

Caresses of the sea...

...Never knowing what tomorrow will be!

Striving for love,

Decorative elements lovely tuned

For the perfect actress in role

To strive for your love

Striking the oyster from above.

He waits calmly-he's not alive (the oyster), mind you!

Not alive this picture, too!

But this is the conceiving of grace

When I strive for love

In an (i)mortal place;

Just an intention - in its premature state

Of demanding your pardon

If you neglected me too much!

In this place, contrarily, it's a Polar Cold

Stones could crack

But keep your head!

24th of January 2013 (after three days of -20 °C)

Deep Chakra

There was a time when

We thought life is safe,

We thought we were good

But challenges proved us otherwise.

Where did I lost my prone

«Hello, I am connected:

My mind with my soul.»

I feel the present slips away

On back doors opened towards the past;

Some time we've lost

And isn't mine.

I beg your pardon, Oh my God,

To save us from Chimers

That dance embraced in me and them

To the finality that the Ring of the Lord

Gets lost.

In my repose, I'm pointing

With the finger meaning ONE

And just when I hear the echo of «Amen»

I lose my balance and I fall again deep

In the Bermuda of the Rationality Sleep.

The engines roam in mental structures

The voices cut to pieces my CD's

I beg your Pardon, Oh my Lord,

Take all the pieces and

Make again a real ME.

Poems translated from Romanian

(«Fragments»-Reflection Publishing, 2012)

The taming of Nature

I wish you hold me from falling

In the green, windy landscape

When my mind is falling from fairy tales

In a safari

With savage leaves dancing in the wind.

When the unlimited ground of imagination

Doesn't fit under the horizon,

Estranged, perceiving the World

That dances around me

Wild, like on another Earth,

I call you with a thought

To catch my waste

And make me continue my walk singing,

To tell me that the World is round again

And that everything that I imagined in my dream

Is standing also under my step

Waiting patiently my way to retake.

Everything I described - I was maybe

Laughing and joking,

Tell me! Was it your own design, too?

Just to make us meet

Under the sun eclipse,

Under this «ring of fire»,

Just to let us borrowed

By the World splendor?

21 may 2012

Don't stop the rain

Don't stop the wet silence

With drops of rain banging in the window,

Time teaches me how to stop whipping

To leave tomorrow proudly

Towards a new horizon.

Break downs, intersections,

Falling in the lake that spread

Slowly in my back, healing the pain.

Today I stay on its edges and cry

About the time when your departure snipped

The clock of our love.

Yesterday, in snowing willow

We followed the same dream,

But what is yesterday, when even time

Is a playful runner and mean.

Don't stop the wet silence

Drops of rain on my thought

Slowly infuse,

The sadness and loneliness

Are fading, are dying...

Your firm power camouflages

In a prayer with transparent

Mantras of rain

That flow from my hands.

My thought is a wooden Buddha

On which the water flows in torrents

From the house's pipes, tock, tock,

The Saints are singing led by the rain.

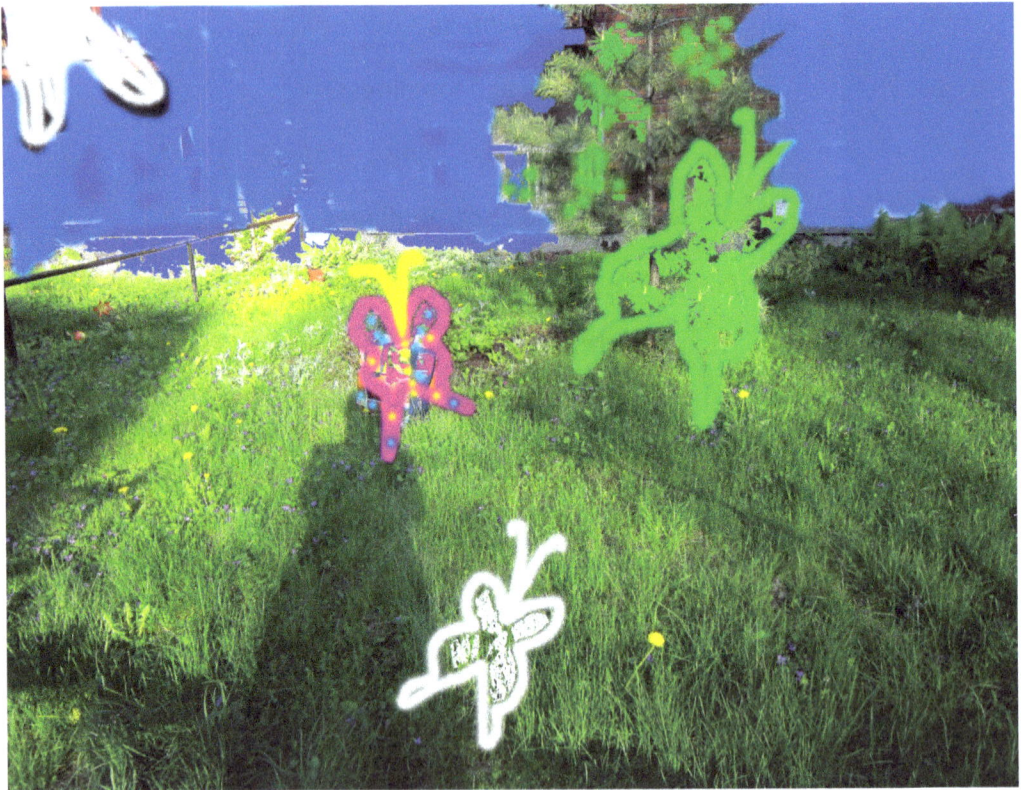

Butterflies and my shadow at 3010 Goyer, *photography (2012)*

Your reflection

The reflection of a thought

In the deep crystal of time

Revolting a butterfly in your temple

Who learns to fly towards the sun,

Stopped in time by the convex mirror

Which is my eye-and I look at you

And I tell you: "In me you shall deposit

Your hot butterflies of desire,

I, being like a screen

Before their flight becomes ashes

In their revolving flight approaching the sun.»

The green of silent grass

On the cutting edge of unknown moments

Is born in my soul

Becoming your shadow...

The freshness of stars,

The glass of water,

After your worried run.

Dedication

Steadings still in the wind,

The sea is dying them slowly

But there's no pain,

The same my thought to you,

Unchanged, but more and more pale

Is trembling in the sunset calling.

Why didn't you come today

When our island

Is merging with the land

And unknown footsteps print the wilderness

That once was our Eternal Saint Land.

Salty the lips of our stone idols

From our island

They carry on their feet

The weaving water pots

In the hit of the summer,

Burning fire in their hands of stone.

Human idols, virgins,

How far from the crowds

How far from tasting the freshness

Bighting the fruits

Which hang forbidden

In the mysterious gardens

Of your love.

The sea is falling asleep,

A warm breeze is turning me

On my other side, complete,

I dreamt that I shouted at the sky

Calling your name through the horn prolonged

From my mouth directly to God,

Now in dim-light,

Now in dim-light...

Heron, *ink and acrylics on rice paper (2010)*

The Heron

I dreamt long, long ago, so far

A big white bird, without a name

Which asked me to choose

Between stillness and flight.

I couldn't answer straight
And then I took a feather
And I painted the bird
Still, in one leg,
In a still life
With a still waterfall
And with a pine in which
The wind stood still.

But painting and painting
I was rotating the feather
And from its flight,
The characters of the lines
Where landing one by one
On the paper
The colorful flight from a feather
As one thousand flying birds.

The thought was appearing
In the dim-opened eyes
My hand was sliding on the paper,
The painting was emerging
From the flying imagination.

This is how I found the answer
For flight and stillness.

Japanese landscape, *ink and watercolor on rice paper (2010)*

Japanese landscape

A ream vibrated
Hitting water monotone
At the pontoon
And the sound carried by the wind
Is heard equally in all this landscape
In which
Every sound is heard equally
In this landscape.

Such a big silence...
Therefore the bell that rings at the door
Is heard on the rocks, on the sea
And runs in circles on the valley.

Every rock moved
By a frog or a crow
Runs fast with its sound
Circling the landscape
From side to side.

I signed this landscape
And the sound of the pen
Was heard from horizon to horizon.

Waterfalls

I didn't know I was crying

But I was whipping waters of a blue winter.

Nobody was nearby,

Just waters softly sliding

And branches with dying leaves

Banging in the wind.

My breath was heard in waterfalls

And the soft whisper of springs-

-I wasn't thinking that I was crying,

Inside of me was the waterfall,

But I was sitting on its edge

At the edge of my thought.

Spring Grace

Three carnations

Enrolled in a row, as a Salute,

Gracefully standing

One, two, three,

In a pottery pot.

The smallest, further,

Gets her head out as an emotion,

The middle one Is spring again

And the biggest is a summer day, already.

One, two, three,

A baguette if you take

You make them appear again

Tomorrow unchanged and free.

Nightingales

Do not sleep! Sweet nightingales
Raven light spread ahead
With their tails brushing the moon
Singing Hum Hummara Hum.

Three descending on a brunch,
Two of which just reached your arm
Singing in your ear: I'm here!
Once upon a time... I'm near!

Hum Hummara Hum they sing,
We are bringing to you Spring,
In our eyes you can see
Who loves you for Eternity!

Do not sleep! White night, they sing
Listen to the joy that brings
Morning glory on our wings,
Hum Hummara and the moon
Gloomy past the shades of trees
Loosing herself in the fairy of the melody.

Trees at sunset at Goyer 3010, *photography (2011)*

Remembering a berry-tree

It was a lazy tree -

- It was not moving anywhere else, in any season.

But what grubs where climbing his wood!

And what butterflies were eating his berries!

And what juicy berries he had,

White and plump

And what ants were not afraid

To conquer him, to tease him!

It wasn't tall, but full of bumps,

With its branches carrying fruits and flowers plenty

Easy to climb -

- Children with pans or without

Were coming to pick it.

The old berry had a wood

Very good to be drawn -

- Leonardo da Vinci would agree

His tingled branches and knots

Were giving him the right to be

An Old Biblical Tree,

Or even Vedant,

The way he was serving

Next to the Church in Lime,

Next to all Saints and Ancestors I have.

Table of Contents

Previous published book by Eva Halus

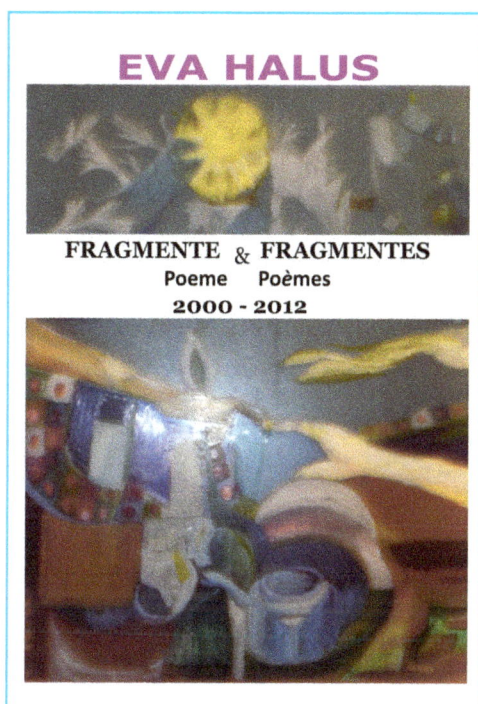

Fragmente/Fragmentes (Poeme/Poemes) 2000-2012
(Multiple Languages: Romanian and French)

ISBN-10: 193662916X
ISBN-13: 978-1936629169

Book size: 0.2 x 7.3 x 9.5 inches
Published by Reflection Publishing (September 19, 2012)

Reflection Publishing
P.O. Box 2182
Citrus Heights, California 95611-2182
E-mail: info@reflectionbooks.com
Tel/message: (916) 604-6707
www.reflectionbooks.com

www.ingramcontent.com/pod-product-compliance
Lightning Source LLC
Chambersburg PA
CBHW050355100426
42739CB00015BB/3401